JOSEPH
The Epic Poetic!
the Bible story of Joseph in verse

by

Jo Johnson

This book belongs to:

Published by Rosebine Press
www.rosebinepress.com

Copyright © 2024 Jo Johnson
Illustrations copyright © Jo Johnson 2024

Jo Johnson has asserted his rights
Under the Copyright, Designs and Patent Act
1988, to be identified as the author and illustrator of this
Work

All rights reserved.
No part of this book may be reproduced in any form or by any electronic or mechanical means, including information storage and retrieval systems, without written permission from the author, except for the use of brief quotations in a book review.

A catalogue record for this book is available from the British Library.

ISBN 978-1-7397443-4-2

Illustrations by Jo Johnson
Cover Design by Jo Johnson

Paperback First Edition

TEN FACTS ABOUT JOSEPH AND HIS FAMILY

1. Joseph lived in a tent, in the land of Israel.
2. Joseph's dad was Jacob.
3. He was a shepherd.
4. Jacob married Leah ...
5. *and* ... her younger sister Rachel!
6. Rachel was Joseph's mum.
7. Jacob loved her very much, but Rachel died when Joseph's little brother Benjamin was only just born.

8. Leah was mum to ten boys*.
9. They were Joseph's step-brothers.
10. They were nasty to Joseph because he was Jacob's best-loved son.

Now turn the page and read the story:
JOSEPH - THE EPIC POETIC !

```
         * The simplified version!
Read the full story in the first book of the Bible:
           Genesis chapters 37 - 50.
```

The Epic Poetic Story of Joseph!

Jacob gave Joseph,
the son that he favoured,
A beautiful, gorgeous,
fantabulous coat;
In colours abundant
so finely was tailored–
It struck a distinctive,
exceptional note.

Alas, this made his brothers sad -
all ten of them got awfully mad;
And when their deeds were very bad -
Joseph went and told their dad.

His brothers' sheaves bowed down so low!
It was the most perplexing riddle.

When Joseph told them of this thing,
They said "We take this very sore;
In your _dreams_, you'll be our king!"
And him they hated even more.

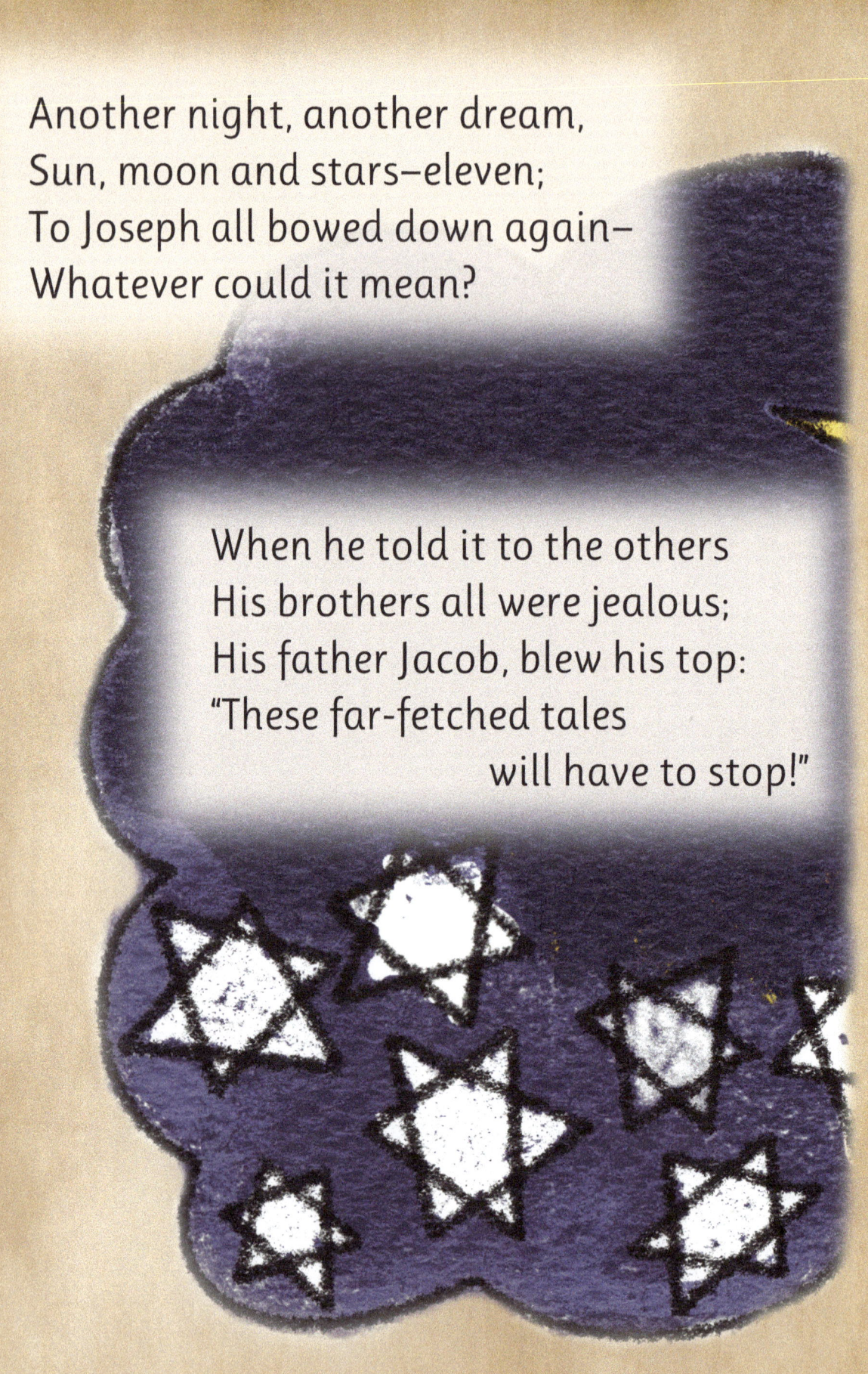

Another night, another dream,
Sun, moon and stars—eleven;
To Joseph all bowed down again—
Whatever could it mean?

When he told it to the others
His brothers all were jealous;
His father Jacob, blew his top:
"These far-fetched tales
 will have to stop!"

The brothers had to feed their flock
In Shechem's field, just north of
                             Hebron
So, Jacob sent his favourite son
His brothers and the sheep, to seek.

Joseph walked for miles and miles
O'er fences, fields and many stiles,
He searched in every but and ben,
But found no sign of sheep or men.

A stranger with a piercing stare,
Found Joseph searching everywhere;
"I'm looking for my brothers ten"
"Have you seen them in the glen?"

"Yes" said the man, "I heard them say,
We'll stop at Dothan on the way";
So, on he marched o'er country vast,
Until he found them all, at last.

His brothers saw him in the distance,
And wickedly, they vowed to slay him:
"Let's put an end to his existence!
Here's this dreamer! Let us kill him!"

"No, no!" said Reuben, "don't do that,
Murder is wicked – it isn't right!"
So, they threw him down an empty well,
Where none would hear him shout and yell.

The brothers were about to eat,
When Ishmael's camels came in sight;
Bold Judah said "Let's sell this dreamer,
And then the money we shall share!"

"That's the answer!" said those rascals,
And pulled up Joe with heedless hurry;
Sold him weeping, to the traders,
For twenty silver coins of money.

When Reuben found poor Joseph gone,
He mourned the foul deed they'd done;
He wished he could have saved his brother–
How now explain this loss to father?

The brothers killed a baby goat
And in its blood, they dipped the coat,
Then sent it home to Jacob with a note.
"Is this your son's nice coat?" they wrote,
And Jacob said with fear and dread,
"Without a doubt, my son is dead."

To comfort him his family tried
But Jacob—he just sobbed and cried;
He said "in mourning for my son, I'll die,
These floods of tears I'll never dry."

To Egypt marched the traders brave,
And sold their wares in the Bazaar;
Along came Captain Potiphar,
And bought young Joseph as a slave.

Potiphar, captain of Pharaoh's guard
Made poor Joseph sweep the yard;
But Joseph had learned to watch and pray;
God gave him strength for each new day.

With Joseph in charge,
everything flourished,
He always made sure
the household was nourished.

With God on his side,
all went to plan,
And Potiphar made him
his right-hand man.

But Potiphar's wife fancied Joseph so manly,
And repeatedly asked him to come to her bed;

She kept Joseph's coat and
made up a story:

"That slave tried to kiss me,
he forced himself on me,
But he ran when I screamed, yes,
I screamed out so loudly!"

And when Potiphar heard it,
he became ever so angry!

He grabbed poor old Joseph,
who was now in disgrace,
And, along with two convicts
sent down from the palace,
He shut him in prison,
with none to console,
And the iron walled darkness
ate into his soul.

But God-fearing Joseph
refused to despair
He immediately made it
a matter of prayer;
And presently,
Joseph made friends with the jailer–
Who put him in charge
of the prisoner's welfare.

Pharaoh's butler and baker
offended him greatly,
(So he sent them to jail
in a raging red fury)
From society royal they
found themselves severed,
'Till the king of all Egypt
their futures decided.

One night these two culprits each had a dream,
But decidedly not about custard and cream!
Afflicted and worried they were when they woke,
They knew it was serious, it wasn't a joke.

To their cell in the morning came Joseph along,
And found them acutely, profoundly harassed;
With concern in his voice he said,
                                                  "what can be wrong,
To make both of you look
                                                  so sad and downcast?"

So, they told him they'd each
                                        had a very strange dream,
And neither had power to uncover the theme;
'Please tell me', said Joseph, 'and God will explain,
I know HE is able, to make it all plain'.

The butler spoke first,
Well, he said he had seen,
Three vine branches hanging
with luscious ripe grapes;
"I squeezed out the wine into
Pharaoh's own cup,
And I gave him the liquor
to drink and to sup.

"Oh, the meaning of this"
said Joseph, "is good,
Three days from today,
from this jail you'll be freed!
When you're back at your job
please tell Pharaoh of me–
I was thrown into prison
for no reason, you see.

The baker, in hope,
now his dream did narrate,
"Three baskets with pastries
and birds on my pate"–
"Oh dear, my good friend,"
Joseph said with dismay,
"In three days, you will die,
I'm so sorry to say."

Sure enough, in three days,
Pharaoh made a great feast,
The butler, (as Joseph foretold)
was released;

But the baker,
in lieu of working with yeast,
Was hanged on a tree
and became –'the deceased.'

Two years later Pharaoh dreamed,
of seven cattle fat,
From the river Nile they rose,
and all green grass devoured;

Then seven skinny cows appeared,
whose appetites were not in doubt,
They gobbled up the other ones –
yet skinny still, remained!

Pharaoh fell asleep again
and had a second vision:
    Seven giant ears of corn,
Upon a single stalk were borne

Then seven tiny scrawny ones appeared,
And swallowed all the jumbo ones –
how weird!

Pharaoh commanded his master magicians
To explain his strange, enigmatic envisions;
But neither enchanter nor wizard unravelled
The mysterious dreams that had Pharaoh baffled.

Just then, the butler recalled he'd forgot,
To speak to his boss about poor Joseph's plight;
So, quickly—he told of his dream in the jail,
Where Joseph its meaning to him did unveil.

Then urgently Pharaoh for Joseph sent,
And told him of animals scrawny and fat;
Good Joseph replied "I only guarantee this–
That God will give you an answer of peace."

This was the answer that calmed Pharaoh's fears:
"Both dreams are one"–and it's not at all mad,
"Two sevens of cows and two sevens of ears,
Is two sevens of years, first good and then bad".

So, Joseph suggested
that Pharaoh so noble,
While seven years plenty
were more or less global,
Should gather and store
one fifth of the grain,
To see the whole nation
through the years of no rain.

"Joseph!" said Pharaoh,
"What a grand scheme ingenious!
I'll put you in charge—yes,
we'll do this between us—
My gold chain of office,
round your neck will be thrown,
And you'll only be second
to me on the throne."

BOW THE KNEE!

Then Pharaoh gave Joseph
a noteworthy name,
And on Joseph's neck placed
the king's golden chain,
"Zaph Enath Paneah,
shall you now be called"
(Which means in Egyptian),
"Saviour of the whole World."

BOW THE KNEE!

So all the people
bowed the knee
While Joseph obeyed
the king's decree,
But when the famine
made life tough
Pharaoh said
"now go to Joseph!"

Saviour of The World

Back in Canaan, Joseph's dad,
Heard Egypt still had plenty bread;
That staple was in short supply,
So he sent his sons, some corn to buy–
(But Benjamin he kept at home,
"I'd die" said he, "if harm befell him").

To Egypt's land they took their journey,
With donkeys and cash, across the desert;
And after days of travel weary,
At Joseph's shop arrived at last.

Then Joseph saw them
bow before him
But pretended
not to know them;
'By Pharaoh's life,
you're spies I think!'
And shut them,
three days in the clink.

Then his ten brothers all explained
They were the sons of just one father;
At home they'd left their youngest brother
Because–they said–there's one that's dead!

"Right" said Joseph, "that should clinch it–
Here's how I'll know you're honest men,
Next time you come, you bring young Ben,
Or home you'll go, a journey wasted.

So, from the prison Joseph freed them,
Gave them corn and sent them home;
"Come again and say 'Shalom'–
But when you come again, bring Ben."

Then in Hebrew, Reuben spoke:
"Joseph's blood is now invoked,
I said don't sin against the boy,
To sell him was a cruel ploy."

The brothers stopped on journey back
To feed their donkeys for the night
One found his money in the sack!
It gave them all a dreadful fright.

To Canaan land their weary way they trudged,
And told old Jacob whom they loved;
"Spies! Three days in prison—corn and money,
And Simeon kept in jail! It sure ain't funny."

Then, when their sacks of corn they opened,
Out fell the other bags of money!
Old Jacob shook his head, and said–
"All these things are now against me".

No rain, no crops, all food diminished,
The years of famine took their toll,
The corn they'd bought in Egypt, finished;
They hadn't even one bread roll.

They *needed* dough to make their bread,
So, Jacob said, "go buy more corn;
Cos, if you don't, we'll all be dead",
He chided them, and looked forlorn.

Then Judah laid it on the line,
"The man in Egypt told us straight,
Unless we bring young Benja-mine,
He won't allow us through the gate".

Old Jacob sighed, then gave command:
"Take double money in your hand,
And nuts and honey, spice and myrrh,
A present for the Egyptian ruler."

The brothers took some cinnamon,
And double money in their hand;
And with their brother Benjamin,
They journeyed down to Egypt's land.

When Joseph saw his brother Ben,
And brothers ten had come again
He told his servant, "Bring them in—
I'm going to dine with them at noon."

Unbidden came the thought
 in anxious waves,
That fearsome man is going to
 make us slaves!"

They blurted out:
"We've double money brought";
The servant said
"it's okay–do not be distraught!"

Then Simeon he set free from prison,
And for their feet, gave water in a basin,
And while he fed the donkeys, they got busy,
Unpacked, and made their present ready.

At noon, the mighty ruler did arrive
And kindly asked them how they fared,
But in particular, he asked,
"Is the old man still alive?"

But when he saw young Benjamin,
A heartfelt sob could barely hide;
Went quickly to his room and cried,
Washed his face, and came again.

'Set on bread! Let's eat' he said,
And sat each one in birthday order;
At this strange thing, they were amazed—
But soon relaxed with mirth and banter.

So, after dinner,
          Joseph bade his lackey,
The brothers' sacks
            with grain fill up–
"As much as they can carry
            –plus their money;
And in the youngest brother's –
           hide my silver cup."

At morning light, they turned around
Began their journey, homeward bound;
Then Joseph ordered, "Up! Pursue!"
"Now all my dreams are coming true".

The servant when he caught them, said
"Folks, this is some return for bread;
To steal my master's cup of silver—
That surely wasn't very clever?"

"Oh, no!" they spluttered, "God forbid,
We would not want to steal your kit!
Go right ahead and search our stuff,
You'll never find it in your puff."

So, from the eldest to the youngest,
He searched and poked in every pack;
And with a flourish, found at last
The silver cup–in Benjy's sack!

In shock and discombobulation
They tore their jackets, ripped their clothes;
And to the city all did hasten
To face the wrath which they'd exposed.

To Joseph's house they all returned
And saw him standing grim and stern;
Each one bowed low upon the ground–
'WHAT IS THIS DEED YOU'VE DONE?' he said.

So, Judah said "what can we say'?
God has found us out this day;
If we cannot clear our sin
You must make us slaves and bondmen."

"Oh no", said Joseph, "God forbid,
All the rest will I exclude,
Except the pup who stole my cup;
I'll keep that knave, to be my slave."

Then up spoke Judah "Oh my lord,
Please don't be angry, take on board—
You asked us of our little brother
The only one left of his mother.

And then you said, 'don't re-appear
Unless you bring your brother here.'
But we said "sorry, not a chance,
On that our dad would look askance.

Later, when the grain was finished
(Depleted, gone, and not replenished);
Dad said again 'go buy some food'
But then, we said, 'we must take Ben'.

'I'll keep him safe', I promised Dad,
And undertook to guard the lad;
I told him 'I will bear the blame forever,
If we don't return together'.

'Alright, but if you're telling me a lie';
Said Dad, 'I'll not survive–in fact I'll die!
To lose one son was bad enough
But two would be extremely tough'".

Judah paused; then firmly said
"Let Ben go home to see his father
And take me as your slave instead;
My solemn promise I must honour."

Those noble words broke Joseph's heart,
He could no longer act a part;
He told his servants, "Leave, begone!
I want to speak with them alone."

They, gathered round him, as he said,
"Yes, I'm your brother whom you sold!
Please, don't be sad—though it was bad,
God made it good—so let's be glad!

He sent me here to save your lives
Go home my brothers, tell your wives:
This famine lasts for five more years—
(To stay at home would end in tears).

Hurry now – go tell my father,
God has made me Egypt's ruler;
Come and bring your families too,
I will nourish, feed and keep you."

Joseph wept on Benjamin's neck,
And Ben was just as much a wreck;
Joe kissed his brothers with a smile,
And after that they talked a while.

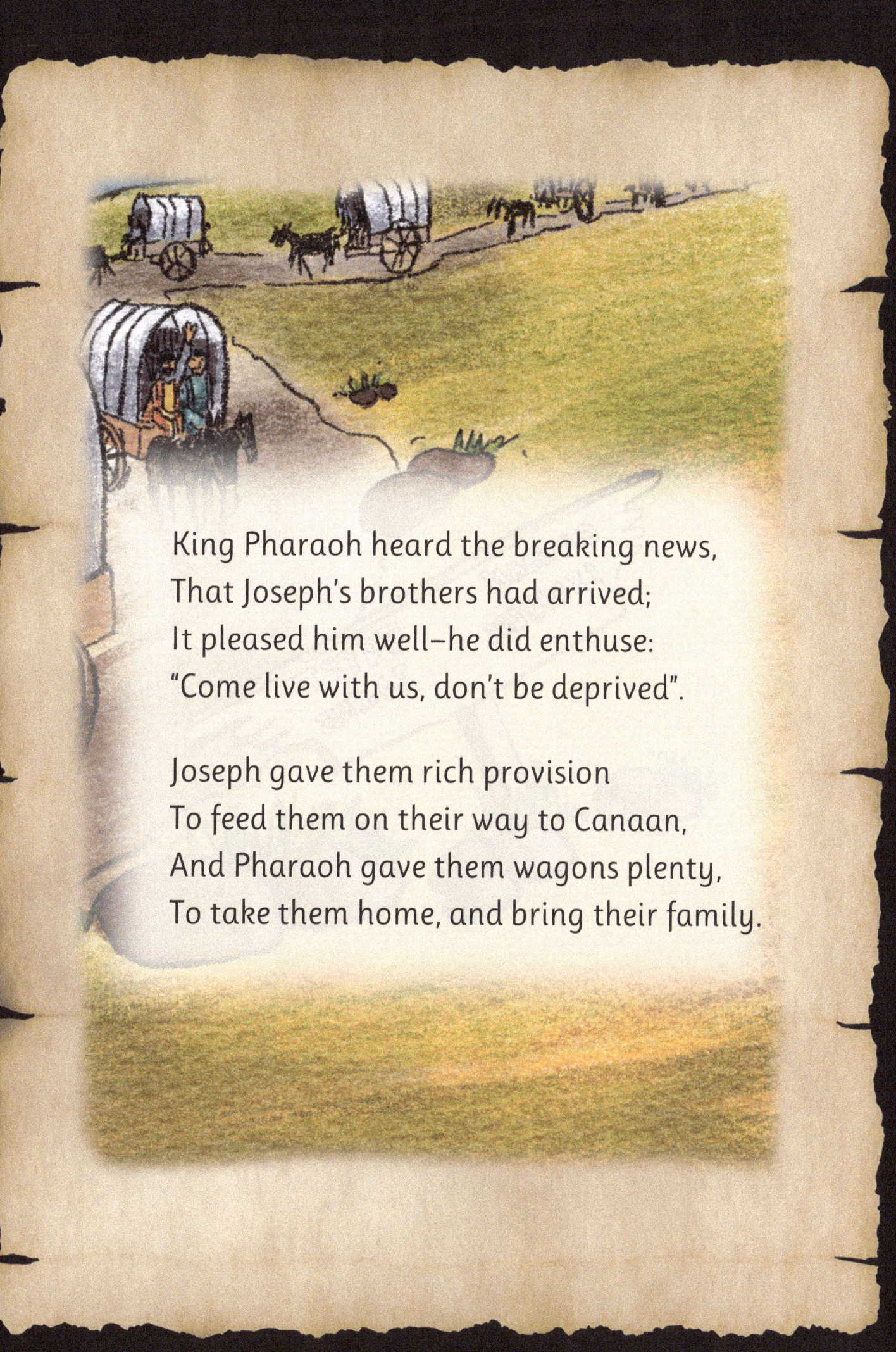

King Pharaoh heard the breaking news,
That Joseph's brothers had arrived;
It pleased him well—he did enthuse:
"Come live with us, don't be deprived".

Joseph gave them rich provision
To feed them on their way to Canaan,
And Pharaoh gave them wagons plenty,
To take them home, and bring their family.

The brothers told their dear old father
"You won't believe it—Egypt's ruler—
That man to whom we bowed, obedient!
Is your son Joseph—Pharaoh's regent!"

Jacob fainted, then revived,
He saw the wagons and believed;
It is enough", was his reply
I'll see him now, before I die.

God to Israel in the night
Said "Jacob, Jacob, do not fear,
Go to Egypt, it's alright,
You and yours, I'll bring back here.

From Beersheba, Jacob went
And came to Egypt with his tent;
All his family kept alive
Altogether, seventy-five.

From chariot royal, Joseph stepped,
Fell on Jacob's neck and wept;
Tears of joy and not of sadness,
Thrilling moment, full of gladness.

So Jacob came, through thick and thin,
To the haven God supplied;
And in the chosen land of Goshen,
Lived in peace, until he died.

The End!

Read the whole story of Joseph in the first book in the Bible:

Genesis chapters 37 - 50

More great Bible Stories:

OLD TESTAMENT

The Story of Abraham and Isaac: Genesis chapter 22
The Story of Jacob and Esau: Genesis chapters 25:19-34 & 27
The Story of Moses: Exodus chapters 1:8-22 & 2:1-21
The Story of Joshua and Jericho: Joshua chapter 6:1-25
The Story of Gideon: Judges chapters 6 & 7
The Story of Samson: Judges chapters 13 - 16
The Story of David and Goliath: 1 Samuel chapter 17
The Story of Elijah: 1 Kings chapters 17 - 19:1-21; 2 Kings 2:1-14
The Story of Elisha and Naaman: 2 Kings chapter 5
The Story of Esther: Esther chapters 1 - 10
The Story of Daniel in the Lion's Den: Daniel chapter 6
The Story of Jonah and the Whale: Jonah chapters 1 - 4

NEW TESTAMENT

The Story of Jesus Birth: Luke chapter 1:36-38,
Matthew chapter 1:18-25, and Luke chapter 2: 1-20
The Story of five loaves and two fish: Mark chapter 5:30-44
The Story of a blind man: John chapter 9
The Story of a storm and a man in a cemetery: Luke 8:22-39
The Story of Lazarus: John chapter 11:1-44
The Story of the crucifixion of Jesus: John chapters 18 & 19
The Story of the Empty tomb: Luke chapter 24
The Story of Stephen: Acts chapter 7
The Story of how Peter escaped from prison: Acts chapter 12:1-17
The Story of Paul, Silas and the earthquake: Acts chapter 16:11-40
The Story of a Shipwreck: Acts chapter 27 and 28:1-10

Also by Jo Johnson:

Cursive Writing Workbook for Kids

Available on Amazon

Other books by Jo Johnson can be found at
www.rosebinepress.com